Primary Science

Seasons and Living Things 1-3

Contents

Other books available in this series include:
Plants and Animals
Earth, Sun, and Stars
Heat, Light, and Sound

Authors
Edward Ortleb
Richard Cadice
Nancy McRee

Artist
Don O'Connor

Managing Editor
Kathy M. Hilmes

Copyright © 1988
Milliken Publishing Company
a Lorenz company
P.O. Box 802
Dayton, OH 45401-0802
www.LorenzEducationalPress.com

MP3313

Seasons and Living Things

This book is a complete teaching tool that, with no preparation, teachers can use with student participation. By distributing duplicates of the pages, teachers can be accompanied by the class as they develop the study. Students complete the exercises to develop their understanding of the subject.

Seasons and Living Things has been prepared by an outstanding authority in the field of science. It offers a ready-made, curriculum-oriented package that is directed to children in the primary grades.

Page 1—The Sun and the Seasons
Concept: The earth's four seasons are caused by the fact that the earth revolves around the sun.

Background Information As the earth revolves around the sun, the angle at which the sun's rays strike the earth changes. This, plus the length of time the sun shines each day, causes the earth to have seasons.

When the Northern Hemisphere of the earth is slanted towards the sun, it experiences summer. During the summer, the days are longer because the sun shines for a long time. The sun's rays are also aimed more directly at the earth, which causes the temperature to be warm.

When the Northern Hemisphere is slanted away from the sun, it experiences winter. During the winter the earth receives only the indirect rays of the sun, and only for a short time.

In the spring and fall, the Northern Hemisphere is slanted neither towards nor away from the sun, which creates a temperature that is neither very warm nor very cold.

The Northern and Southern Hemispheres are called temperate zones because they have four distinct seasons. The Southern Hemisphere has its season opposite to the Northern Hemisphere.

Some areas of the earth, like the tropics, have warm weather all year because the sun shines for a long period of time each day and is directly overhead. Some places, like the North and South Poles are cold most of the year because they receive only indirect sun rays. **Answers** 1) spring, fall; 2) equator; 3) no

Additional Activities 1) Have students study a globe and locate where they live. Ask them if they live closer to the poles or to the equator. 2) Have students find out which months are spring, summer, fall, and winter in places south of the equator.

Page 2—The Earth in Spring
Concept: Spring begins in late March and lasts until late June.

Background Information Because the Northern and Southern Hemispheres are temperate zones, they have four well-defined seasons. About March 21, the sun is directly over the equator, which causes the temperate zones to experience equal periods of day and night. This time, when the day and night each last twelve hours, is called the vernal equinox. The vernal equinox begins the spring season, which lasts until about June 22. The daylight hours become longer as spring progresses, and the temperature becomes warmer. These conditions cause seeds to germinate, shrubs to grow, and trees to bud. Animals that hibernate during the winter also become more active. **Answers** 1) yes; 2) yes; 3) buds

Additional Activities 1) Have students make a list of games and sports people play in spring. 2) Ask students to find out which month is called the "windy month," which month is called the "rainy month," and which month is called the "hot month."

Page 3—The Earth in Summer
Concept: Summer is the warmest season of the year.

Background Information Summer begins about June 22. The first day of summer is called the summer solstice. It is the longest day of the year.

In summer, the sun is directly over the Tropic of Cancer. Because of this, the Northern Hemisphere receives more heat and light energy from the sun. The summer season is characterized by great activity and growth in both plants and animals. **Answers** 1) yes; 2) warm; 3) leaves

Additional Activities 1) Have students make a list of the games and sports people play in the summer. 2) Ask students to find out what season it is in Argentina when it is summer in the United States.

Page 4—The Earth in Fall
Concept: The weather becomes cooler in the fall, which begins about September 23.

Background Information Fall is the season of the year in the temperate zone that begins about the 23rd of September. At this time, the sun is directly over the equator. This causes an equal period of daytime and nighttime (12 hours each). In fall, the daylight hours become progressively shorter and the temperature becomes cooler. These seasonal changes are reflected in the activities of plants and animals. **Answers** 1) the same as; 2) no; 3) nests

Additional Activities 1) Have students make a list of the games and sports people play in fall. 2) Ask students to collect colorful fall leaves. Press them between wax paper to preserve them.

Page 5—The Earth in Winter
Concept: Winter is the last season of the year. It begins about December 22.

Background Information The last season of the year is a period of cold temperatures in the Northern Hemisphere. Winter begins about December 22. The first day of winter is called the winter solstice. It is the shortest day of the year. At this time, the sun is directly over the Tropic of Capricorn in the Southern Hemisphere. Because of this, the Northern Hemisphere receives less light energy and heat energy from the sun. Winter is characterized by short daylight hours and cold temperatures. Plant and animal activity and growth continue at a very slow rate during winter. **Answers** 1) no; 2) more; 3) leaves

Additional Activities 1) Have students make a list of the games and sports people play in the winter. 2) Ask students to research snowflakes.

Page 6—Clothing During the Seasons
Concept: People wear different kinds of clothing in different seasons.

Background Information Students have learned what the earth is like during the different seasons. They will use what they have learned to show what kinds of clothes people wear during spring, summer, fall, and winter.

Additional Activities 1) Discuss with students what kind of fabric winter and summer clothes might be made of. 2) Have students research the kinds of clothes people in extremely hot and extremely cold climates wear.

Page 7—Plants in Spring
Concept: In spring, buds begin to grow and plants begin to bloom.

Background Information Living things become active in the spring. The sun shines more brightly and for a longer period of time each day than in winter. When plants receive warm air and sunshine, they begin to grow again after the winter period of dormancy.

Spring air smells sweet and fresh. Ice and snow that have melted supply the soil with moisture. The ground is warm, soft, and moist, making spring an ideal time for planting. **Answers** 1) warm air, sunshine; 2) May; 4) green

Additional Activities 1) Have students make a list of flowers that bloom in spring. 2) Ask students to find out about the length of days in spring compared to winter. 3) Plant some seeds in containers and watch them grow.

Page 8—Plants in Summer
Concept: Plants grow most quickly during summer.

Background Information Summer is the best growing season. The sun shines brightly for a long period of the day, causing warm temperatures. Plants grow most quickly in the warm sunshine and air. In summer, trees have all their leaves, fruit trees bear fruit, and grass grows rapidly.

The very warm temperatures of summer bring the threat of dryness, so frequent watering of plants is essential to offset the rapid rate of evaporation caused by the heat of the sun. **Answers** 1) sun, air; 2) June; 4) summer

Additional Activities 1) Have students make a chart of flowers and fruits that flourish in summer. 2) Have students experiment with plants. Provide some plants with both water and sunlight, some with just water, and some with just sunlight. Have students record their observations of the plants. 3) Discuss how to identify poison ivy.

Page 9—Plants in Fall
Concept: In the fall, plants change and prepare for winter.

Background Information Fall weather causes a dramatic change in plants. In some areas, the leaves of trees change color and fall to the ground. Many plants end their growing seasons with the production of seeds. These seeds are carried by the wind to different areas.

Fall is different in different parts of the world. Regions near the tropics have flowers that bloom throughout the fall, and the leaves of trees do not change color as they do in the northern regions. Regions near the polar zones have a short, quickly changing fall season, and an early winter. **Answers** 1) color, fall; 2) November; 3) no

Additional Activities 1) Have students make a chart of flowers that bloom in fall. 2) Ask students to research different ways in which seeds are scattered from place to place. 3) Have students collect various kinds of seeds and compare their appearances.

Page 10—Plants in Winter
Concept: Plants are dormant, or resting, during the winter.

Background Information In winter, the air is very cold and snow normally covers the ground for a long time. The snow often acts as a blanket for the roots of many plants. Many plants are able to keep on living, although they rest during the winter and do not grow. Trees wait out the winter season by storing sap in their trunks and roots. When spring comes, the sap will be sent throughout the tree for growth. Regions near the tropics do not normally have snow, though changes in plant life do occur. **Answers** 1) trunk, roots; 3) no

Additional Activities 1) Have students find out what kind of flowers can grow up through the snow. 2) Have students find out why evergreen trees do not lose their needles in the winter.

Page 11—Plants During the Seasons
Concept: Plants look different in the different seasons.

Background Information Students have learned what plants are like in the different seasons. They will use what they have learned to match the right pictures to the right seasons.

Additional Activities 1) Have students research methods for caring for trees during the different seasons.

Page 12—Weather
Concept: Each season has different weather conditions.

Background Information The conditions that cause the four seasons in the temperate zone also produce characteristic weather for each season. Spring is characterized by cool temperatures and windy, rainy weather. Rain clouds may be seen. In summer, the days are bright and sunny, and temperatures are warm or hot. Generally, the only form of precipitation during summer is brief showers. The fall season is characterized by cool temperatures, with some clear, sunny days and some windy, rainy days. Winter is marked by cold temperatures accompanied by gray skies. Snow and sleet are common forms of winter precipitation. **Answers** 1) spring, fall; 2) winter; 3) fall; 4) summer

Additional Activities 1) Have students find out what month has the most rainfall in their area. 2) Have students make a weather chart and keep a record of the weather for one month.

Page 13—Animals in Spring
Concept: Spring is a period of renewed activity for animals.

Background Information The longer hours of daylight and warmer temperatures of spring cause an increase in the activities of animals. For those animals that hibernate, spring is the season to leave hibernation dens and move to summer feeding grounds. Migrating birds return from the warmer regions. Animals that were active all winter become more active. In spring, many animals lay their eggs. Insects, which have been dormant in decaying logs or in soil, rise to the surface and begin breeding. **Answers** 1) squirrel, robin; 2) frog; 3) soil; 4) yes

Additional Activities 1) Obtain some frog or toad eggs and watch them hatch and develop. Have students record their observations. 2) Have students make a list of birds that fly to warmer climates in the winter, but return to students' area in the spring.

Page 14—Animals in Summer
Concept: Most animals are active in summer.

Background Information The summer climate is very favorable for plant and animal life. The longer hours of sunlight and warm temperatures encourage plant growth. Many animals rely on plants and their products for food. Summer is also a period of births and rearing of young. Insects are found in great numbers during summer. **Answers** 1) yes; 2) bees

Additional Activities 1) Ask students to research what adult birds feed their babies. 2) Have students collect some caterpillars and watch them change into pupas and then into moths or butterflies.

Page 15—Animals in Fall
Concept: In fall, animals prepare for winter.

Background Information The decreasing number of hours of daylight and the cooler temperatures of fall, warn living things of the coming winter. Migratory birds flock together and begin their long flight to southern regions. Those animals that remain must prepare for the cold temperatures and lack of a plentiful food supply. The fur of many mammals becomes thicker, and they build up a layer of fat that is utilized during the cold weather. Some animals, like squirrels, store food for later use. Reptiles and amphibians seek crevices and burrows below the frost line to crawl into when temperatures drop. Many insects lay eggs in the fall that will hatch in the spring. **Answers** 1) birds; 2) raccoons; 3) acorns; 4) grasshoppers

Additional Activities 1) Have students research what happens to most insects by the end of fall. 2) Have students find out about the fall color changes by such animals as the arctic fox and the ptarmigan.

Page 16—Animals Get Ready for Winter
Concept: Animals do different things to prepare for winter.

Background Information On page 15, students learned about the different ways animals prepare for winter. They will use what they have learned to match the animal with the activity. **Answers** beaver—eat and get fat; bear—find a place to sleep during cold weather; squirrel—put away seeds, nuts, or other food; rabbit—grow a thick coat that may change colors; duck—fly away to live in a warm place; turtle—go to the bottom of a pond; grasshopper—lay eggs

Additional Activities 1) Have students choose an animal and research the ways in which it prepares for winter.

Page 17—Animals in Winter
Concept: Many animals become inactive in winter, while others remain active throughout the winter season.

Background Information The cold winter season is a resting period for many animals. Insect eggs and larva are safe underground. The raccoon and skunk sleep in warm burrows but are active on the warmer days of winter. Some animals, such as the woodchuck, chipmunk, reptiles, and amphibians truly hibernate in that they do not venture forth until spring. The squirrel is active throughout most of the winter and has a winter den inside a tree cavity. The rabbit's paw prints can be seen in the snow, indicating its activity during the cold. Many birds, such as nuthatches and chickadees, do not migrate and remain active throughout winter in a busy search for food. **Answers** 1) tracks; 2) below, above; 3) no

Additional Activities 1) Have students find out where snakes, foxes, opossums, and honeybees spend the winter. 2) Have students make a list of birds they have seen in the winter.

Page 18—The Life of a Bird
Concept: Birds' lives have a pattern.

Background Information Students have learned about birds' lives. They will use what they have learned to complete the sentences and do the Word Search puzzle. **Answers** worms, insects, migrate, nest, straw, song, red

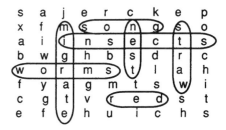

Additional Activities 1) Have students record the morning and evening activities of one of the birds that frequents students' yards or the school yard.

Page 19—Migration
Concept: Some animals travel from place to place according to the season. This is called migration.

Background Information Scientists are undecided as to the exact reason for bird migration. Some possible reasons include a decreasing food supply, change in the length of days, and bi-annual breeding seasons. Some birds, such as the English sparrow, cardinal, crow, and quail do not migrate. Robins may simply migrate from the cities to forests and farm areas 50 to 60 miles away, or they may fly farther south. Some temperate-zone birds, such as hummingbirds, warblers, orioles, and wrens fly to the warm southern states or to tropical regions. Other animals that migrate are bats, salmon, eels, reindeer, and seals. **Answers** 1) yes; 2) 6; 4) seal, salmon

Additional Activities 1) Have students find out about the migration of the eel. 2) Have students research the migration of the lemmings in Norway.

Page 20—Hibernation
Concept: Some animals spend the winter sleeping in protected places. This is called hibernation.

Background Information Changes in daylight length and temperature brought about by the coming of fall is a signal to some animals to prepare for winter. These animals overeat, causing fatty tissue to develop. This fatty material can be drawn on by the body for energy during the winter sleep. Animals that truly hibernate (don't awaken or move about) experience a drop in body temperature and a decrease in the rate of breathing and heartbeat. Water turtles and frogs dig burrows in the mud beneath the water. Snakes and lizards often hibernate in deep rock crevices. Woodchuck and chipmunks sleep in underground burrows that they have prepared. Bats may be found hibernating in hollow logs or caves. **Answers** 1) turtle, frog; 2) bat; 3) snake; 4) bear; 5) no

Additional Activities 1) Have students make a list of some animals found in their state that hibernate. 2) Have students find out about the superstition of Groundhog Day, February 2.

Page 21—Understanding Animals
Concept: Some animals hibernate and some animals migrate during the winter.

Background Information Students have learned about hibernation and migration. They will use what they have learned to circle the names of the animals that hibernate or migrate. **Answers** Hibernate—turtle, bear, groundhog, snake, bat, frog; migrate—duck, seal, elk, butterfly, hummingbird, eagle, salmon

Page 22—Activities in Spring
Concept: Spring is a good time to do many things outdoors.

Background Information Spring is a very busy season for plants and animals (including people). Warm weather, bright sunshine, and longer daytime hours enable people to carry on many outdoor activities. Spring is usually the best time to plant seeds and young plants, and changes in climate offer the opportunity to clean, fix, and paint the house. Recreational activities in spring include games like baseball, tennis, and golf. **Answers** 1) wind; 3) yes

Additional Activities 1) Have students make a list of common activities people do in spring. 2) Ask students to find out about the traditional Maypole celebration.

Page 23—Activities in Summer
Concept: Summer is a good season for many outdoor activities.

Background Information Very warm temperatures and very bright sunlight for a long period of the day make it possible to spend a great deal of time outdoors. Water sports are the most popular outdoor activities during summer. Most people like summer best because it brings vacations and long days for cooking and eating outdoors, firework displays, eating different fruits such as watermelons, cantalopes, peaches, etc. **Answers** 1) weather; (other possible answers: air, water); 3) no

Additional Activities 1) Have students list safety rules concerning water sports. 2) Have students show and tell about their vacations and what they like to do in the summer.

Page 24—Activities in Fall
Concept: In fall, living things change and prepare for winter.

Background Information Many interesting things happen in fall. In some parts of the world, leaves change colors. The air is cool and the sun is not very bright, so people put on warm clothing. Outdoor activities change somewhat because of the change in weather. The days get shorter, and plants and animals prepare for the approaching season of winter. **Answers** 1) leaves, color

Additional Activities 1) Ask students to research how Halloween got started.

Page 25—Activities in Winter
Concept: Because winter is the coldest season, there is little outdoor activity.

Background Information In some parts of the world, winter brings very cold air, ice, and snow. This kind of weather curtails most outdoor activities, except for skating, sledding, and skiing. Short periods of daylight also reduce daytime outdoor activities. Even though some parts of the world do not have ice and snow in winter, temperatures are lower, and daytime hours are shorter. **Answers** 1) ice, cold; 3) yes

Additional Activities 1) Have students make a list of winter activities. 2) Have students find out how snow is made and about the shape of snowflakes.

Page 26—The Seasons
Concept: Many things happen during the four seasons.

Background Information Students have learned about the different things that happen during the four seasons. They will use what they have learned to complete the word search puzzle.

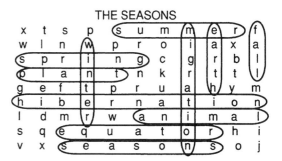

THE SEASONS

Additional Activities 1) Have students create a rebus using one of the words in the word search puzzle.

Page 27—Animals During the Seasons
Concept: Animals do different things in different seasons.

Background Information Students have learned about the things animals do during different seasons. They will use what they have learned to match the pictures to the right seasons. **Answers** Summer: bees, turtle, raccoon, chipmunk; Winter: bear, beaver, mouse, bird

Additional Activities 1) Have students research different species of insects to see how they change with the seasons.

The Sun and the Seasons

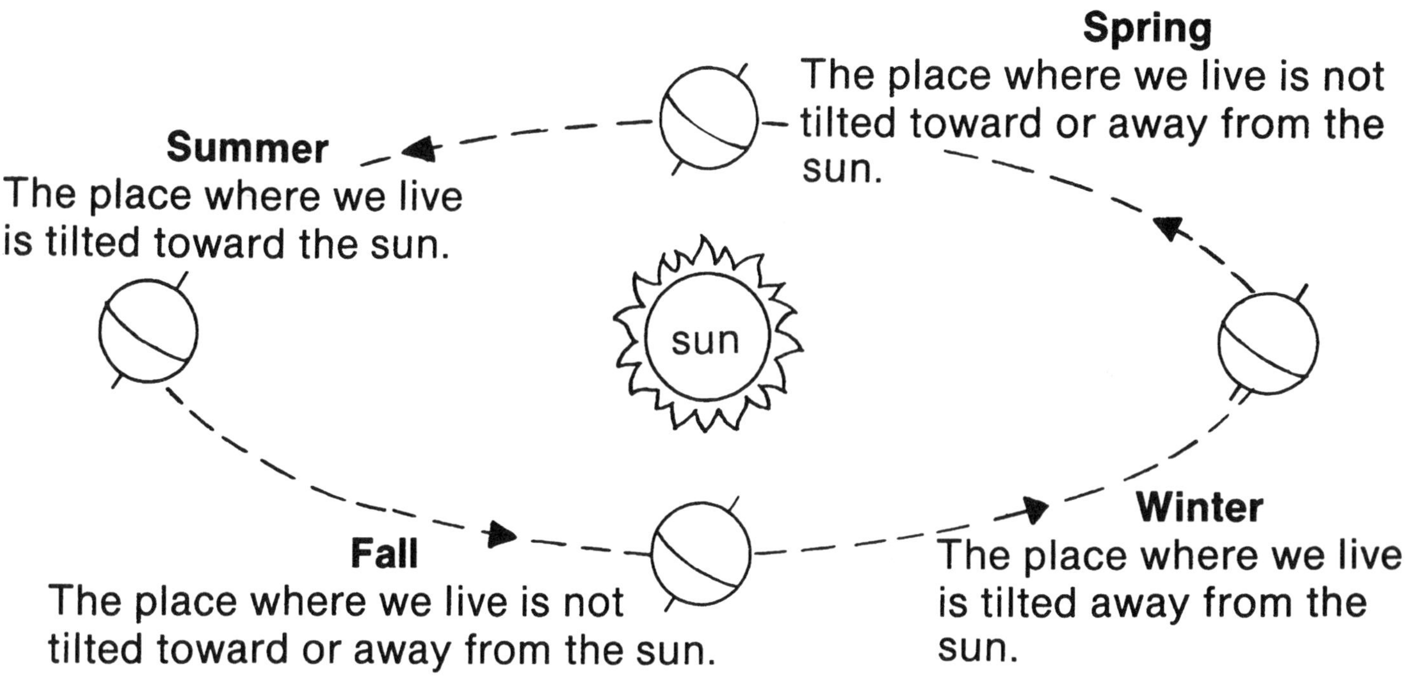

Spring
The place where we live is not tilted toward or away from the sun.

Summer
The place where we live is tilted toward the sun.

sun

Winter
The place where we live is tilted away from the sun.

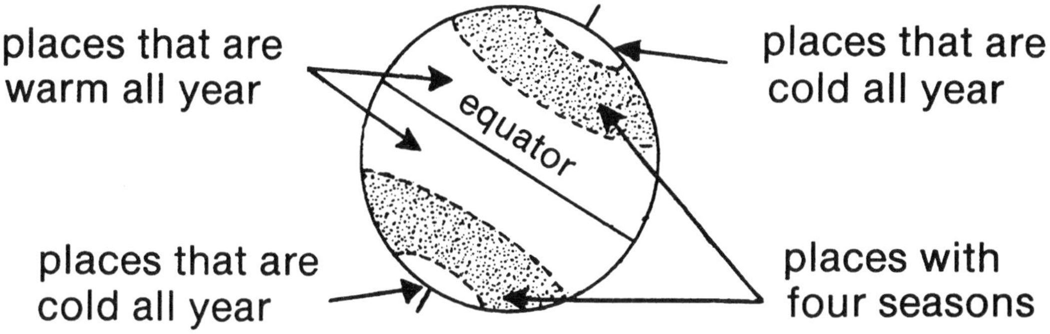

Fall
The place where we live is not tilted toward or away from the sun.

places that are warm all year

places that are cold all year

equator

places that are cold all year

places with four seasons

Some places have four seasons, and some do not.

When People Do Things

rake leaves: _____

build a snowman: _____

plant seeds: _____

go swimming: _____

1. In the top picture, draw a circle around the two seasons where the poles of the earth are not tilted either toward or away from the sun.
2. The bottom picture shows a line that divides the earth in half. This line is called the _____ .
3. Circle your answer: Every place on earth has four seasons.   yes   no

The Earth in Spring

sun-
light

The first day of spring
in the Northern Hemisphere
is about March 21.

length of day ..... 12 hours
length of night ... 12 hours
temperature ...... about 13° C
(55° F)

A Day in Spring

1. Circle your answer: The first day of spring comes near the beginning of the year.   yes   no
2. Draw a red circle around the number of hours in the day and in the night. Are they the same?   yes   no
3. Write the missing word: In spring, many trees have
_____ (grass, buds, paper).
4. Color the bottom picture.

The Earth in Summer

sun-light

The first day of summer
in the Northern Hemisphere
is about June 22.

length of day ..... 14½ hours
length of night ... 9½ hours
temperature ...... about 27° C
(80° F)

A Day in Summer

1. Circle your answer: Summer has more day hours than night hours.
   yes   no
2. Draw a red circle around the temperature in summer.

   Is this temperature warm or cold? _____
3. In the summer, the trees are covered with _____
   (snow, grass, leaves).
4. Color the bottom picture.

The Earth in Fall

sun-light

The first day of fall
in the Northern Hemisphere
is about September 23.

length of day ..... 12 hours
length of night ... 12 hours
temperature ...... about 21° C
(70° F)

A Day in Fall

1. Circle your answer: The number of day hours in fall is
   (more than, less than, the same as) the number of night hours.
2. Draw a line under your answer: The temperature in fall is cold
   enough to ride a sled.   yes   no
3. Write in the missing word: Most birds leave their _____
   (nests, rakes, feet) in fall.
4. Color the bottom picture.

4   Seasons and Living Things.

The Earth in Winter

sun-
light

The first day of winter
in the Northern Hemisphere
is about December 22.

length of day .....   9½ hours
length of night ...   14½ hours
temperature ......   about 2° C
(35° F)

A Day in Winter

1. Circle your answer: Winter has more day hours than night hours.
   yes   no
2. Write in the missing word: In winter, people wear _____
   (more, less) clothes than in summer.
3. Write in the missing word: Most trees do not have their _____
   (bark, roots, leaves) in winter.
4. Color the bottom picture.

Clothing During the Seasons

Draw the clothing you wear in each season.

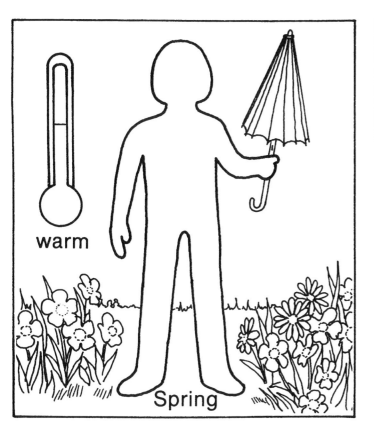

warm

Spring

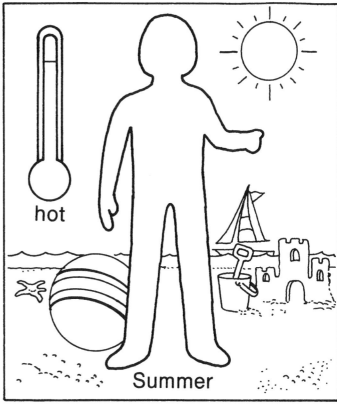

hot

Summer

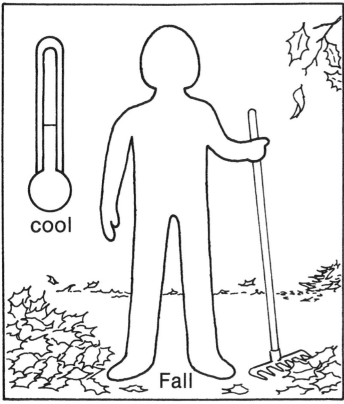

cool

Fall

cold

Winter

Plants in Spring

Warm air and sunshine help plants come to life.

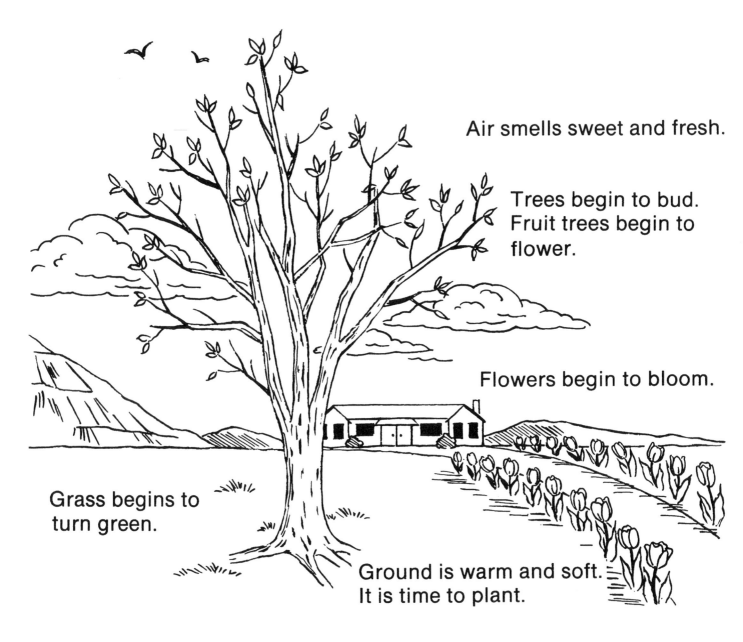

Air smells sweet and fresh.

Trees begin to bud. Fruit trees begin to flower.

Flowers begin to bloom.

Grass begins to turn green.

Ground is warm and soft. It is time to plant.

spring months: March, April, May, June

1. Two things that help plants grow are _____ and
   _____ .
2. Find the list of spring months. Circle the third month of spring.
3. On the back of this paper, tell why spring is a good time to plant things.
4. Grass begins to turn _____ in spring.
5. Color the picture the way you see plants in spring.

Plants in Summer

Summer is the best growing season for plants.

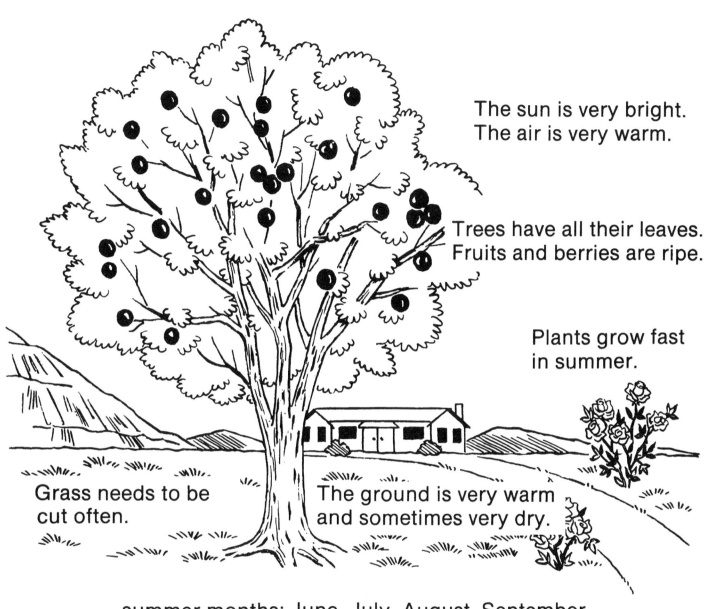

The sun is very bright.
The air is very warm.

Trees have all their leaves.
Fruits and berries are ripe.

Plants grow fast
in summer.

Grass needs to be
cut often.

The ground is very warm
and sometimes very dry.

summer months: June, July, August, September

1. _____ and very warm _____ make summer hot.
2. Find the list of summer months. Circle the month that is both spring and summer.
3. On the back of this paper, tell why plants and trees must be watered in the summer.
4. Circle your answer: Most fruits and flowers are picked in
   spring   summer   autumn   winter
5. Color the picture of plants in summer.

8   Seasons and Living Things

Plants in Fall

Plants begin to change in fall.

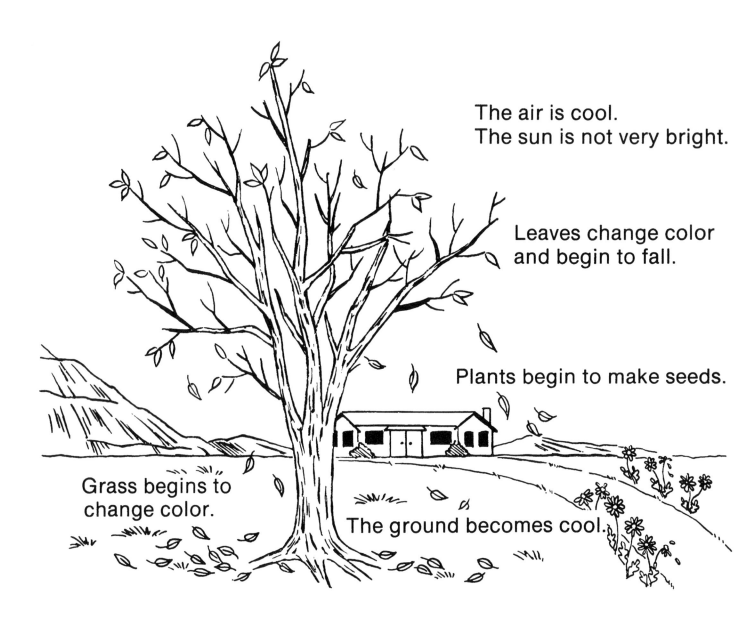

The air is cool.
The sun is not very bright.

Leaves change color
and begin to fall.

Plants begin to make seeds.

Grass begins to
change color.

The ground becomes cool.

fall months: September, October, November, December

1. Two things happen to leaves in fall. They change _____

   and start to _____ .
2. Circle the fall month when you celebrate Thanksgiving Day.
3. Circle your answer: Most plants make flowers in fall.   yes   no
4. Color the picture of plants in fall.

Plants in Winter

> Snow acts as a blanket for many plants.

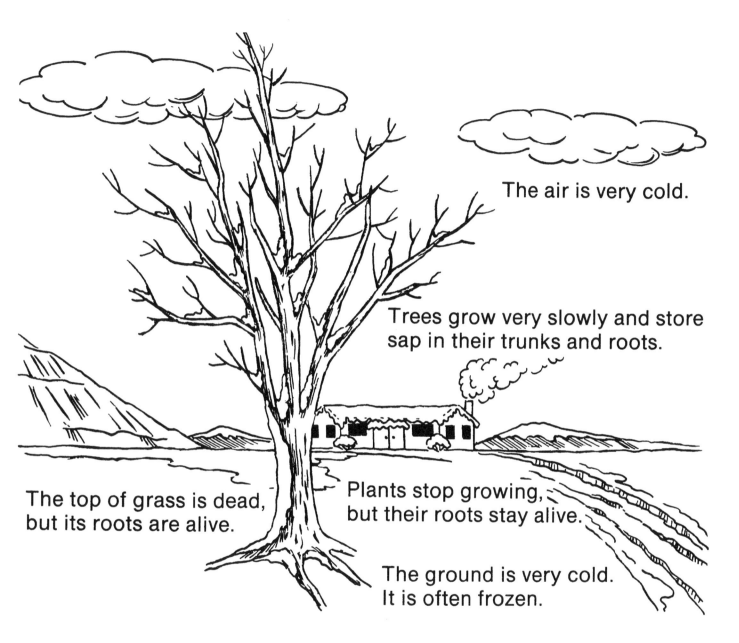

The air is very cold.

Trees grow very slowly and store sap in their trunks and roots.

The top of grass is dead, but its roots are alive.

Plants stop growing, but their roots stay alive.

The ground is very cold. It is often frozen.

winter months: December, January, February, March

1. Two places where trees store sap are in their _____ and _____ .
2. On the back of this paper, tell why a plant may look dead, but it really is not.
3. Circle your answer: Winter is a good time to plant things.   yes   no
4. Color the picture of plants in winter.

Plants During the Seasons

An apple tree looks different each season.
Color the pictures below.
Then cut them out.
Paste them in the right boxes.

Spring	Summer
Fall	Winter

Weather

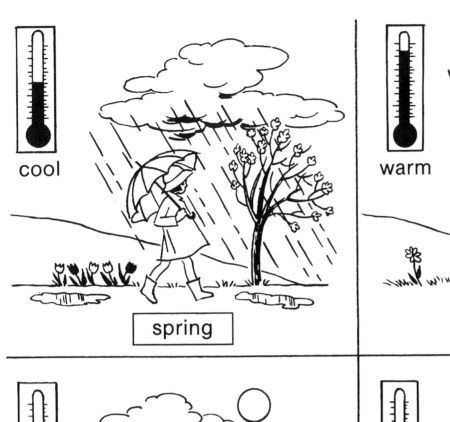

cool

spring

warm

summer

cool

fall

cold

winter

1. Write the names of the two seasons that have temperatures almost alike: _____ and _____ .
2. The skies may be dark and the temperature is cold in _____ .
3. Circle the name of the season in October.
4. Put an X by the name of the season that usually has bright, sunny skies.
5. Color each picture.

Animals in Spring

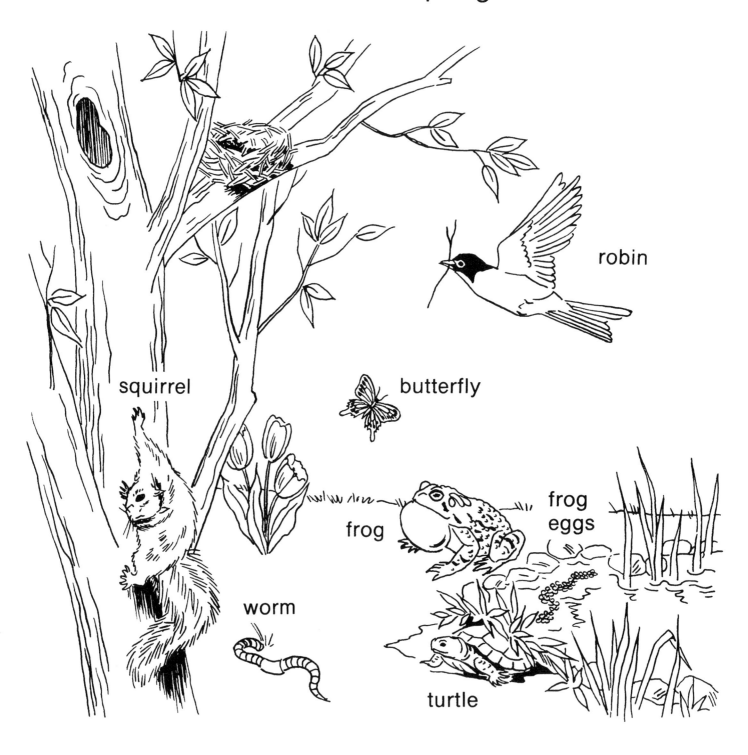

1. Draw a red circle around the animals that live in trees.
2. Draw a blue circle around the animal that lays its eggs in water.
3. Circle your answer: The worm lives in (water, tree, soil).
4. Circle your answer: The butterfly is an insect that flies.   yes   no
5. Color the picture.

Animals in Summer

1. Circle your answer: Baby animals are often seen in summer.
   yes   no
2. Draw a red circle around the insect that flies from flower to flower looking for food.
3. On the back of this paper, tell about some other animals you might see in summer.
4. Color the picture.

Animals in Fall

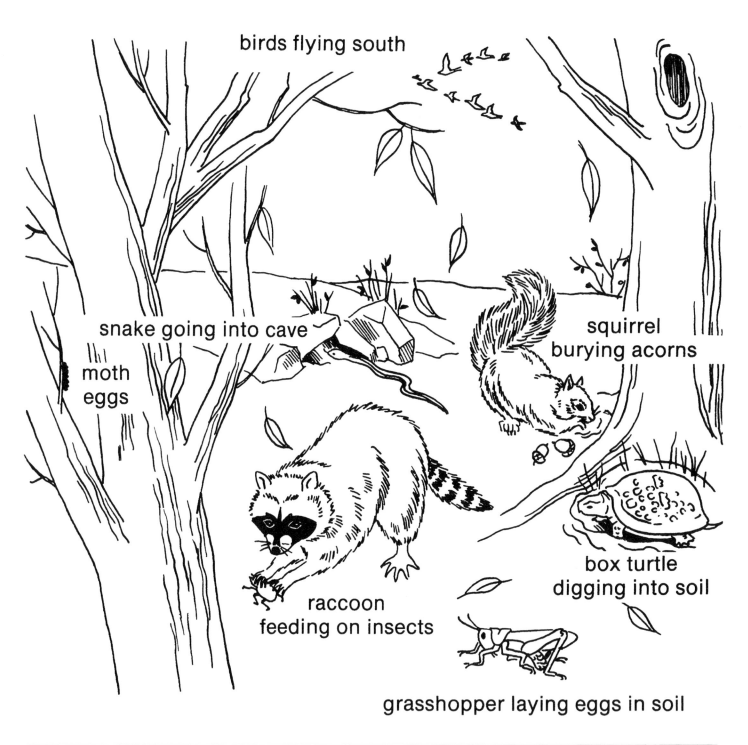

birds flying south

snake going into cave

moth eggs

squirrel burying acorns

raccoon feeding on insects

box turtle digging into soil

grasshopper laying eggs in soil

1. Name the kind of animal that flies south in fall: _____ .
2. What animal with fur likes to eat insects? _____
3. In fall, the squirrel buries _____ for food in winter.
4. The insect that lays its eggs in the soil is a _____ .
5. Color the picture.

Animals Get Ready for Winter

Find out how animals get ready for winter.
Connect the dots.

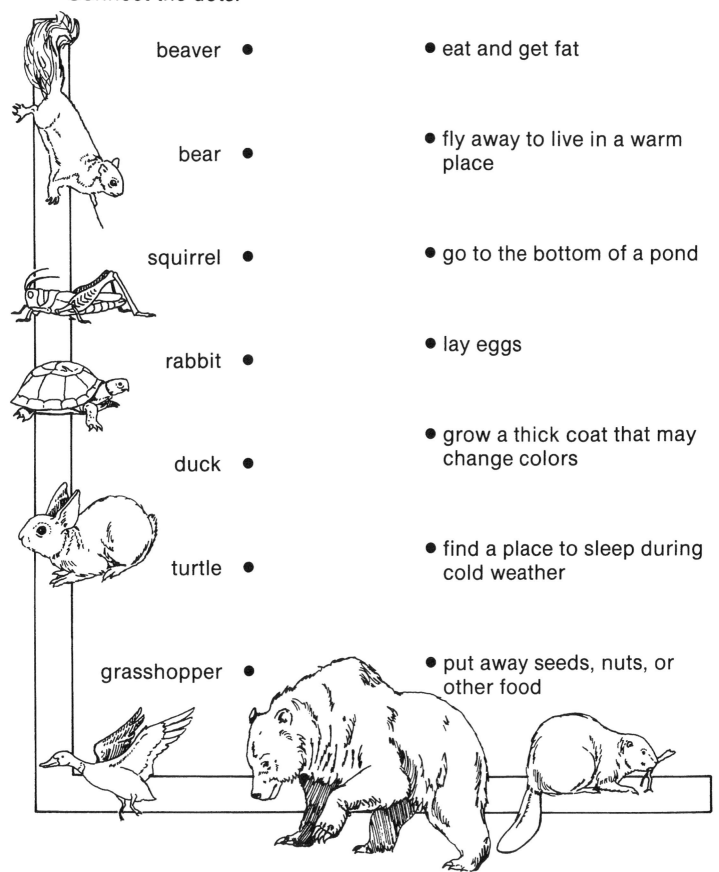

beaver ●

bear ●

squirrel ●

rabbit ●

duck ●

turtle ●

grasshopper ●

● eat and get fat

● fly away to live in a warm place

● go to the bottom of a pond

● lay eggs

● grow a thick coat that may change colors

● find a place to sleep during cold weather

● put away seeds, nuts, or other food

Seasons and Living Things

Animals in Winter

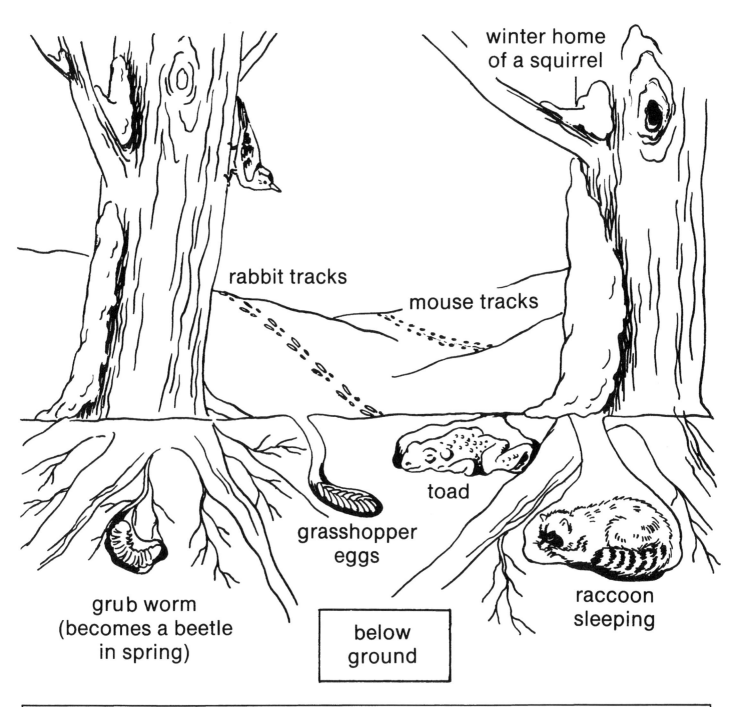

winter home of a squirrel

rabbit tracks

mouse tracks

toad

grasshopper eggs

grub worm
(becomes a beetle in spring)

below ground

raccoon sleeping

1. Sometimes we can not see animals in winter, but we can see their _____ in the snow.
2. Write the correct word: The frog lives _____ (above, below) the ground in winter. The squirrel lives _____ (above, below) the ground in winter.
3. Circle your answer: Rabbits sleep all winter.   yes   no
4. Color the picture.

The Life of a Bird

Word Bank

straw
song
red
worms
migrate
insects
nest

s	a	j	e	r	c	k	e	p
x	f	m	s	o	n	g	s	o
a	i	i	n	s	e	c	t	s
b	w	g	h	b	s	d	r	c
w	o	r	m	s	t	l	a	h
f	y	a	g	m	t	s	w	i
c	g	t	v	r	e	d	s	t
e	f	e	h	u	i	c	h	s

This is the robin that lives in your yard.

Use the word bank to complete the sentences. Then find the words in the puzzle.

The robin eats _____ and _____ .

He must _____ to find this food in the winter.

In the spring, a _____ will be built of mud and _____ .

The robin will sing a happy _____ .

He will shape the mud in the nest with his _____ breast.

18

Migration

| migration — moving from place to place |

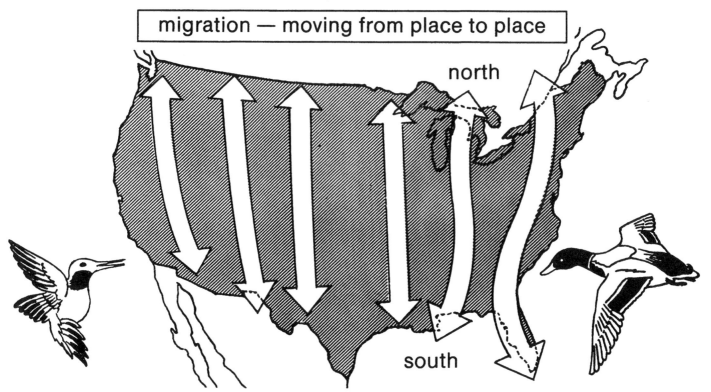

The Main Pathways for Bird Migration in the United States

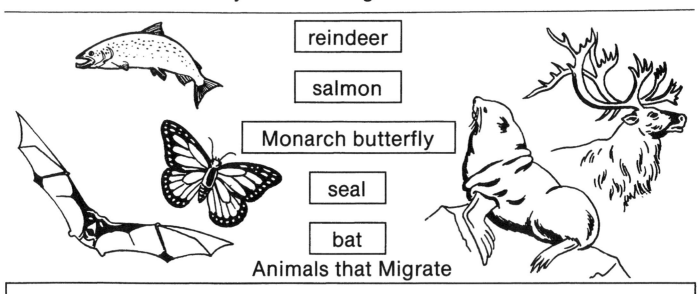

Animals that Migrate

1. Circle your answer: Birds seem to follow certain pathways when they migrate.   yes   no
2. How many main pathways are there for bird migration? _____
   Color the pathway near where you live.
3. Draw a line from the name of each animal to the picture of the animal.
4. In the bottom pictures, circle with red the animals that migrate by swimming.
5. Color the pictures.

Hibernation

hibernation — sleeping through the winter in a protected place

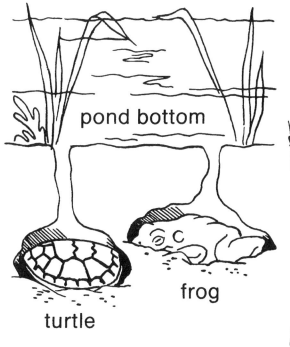

pond bottom

frog

turtle

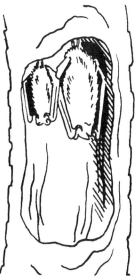

bats in hollow
tree

snake in rocky den

woodchuck or ground hog
in burrow

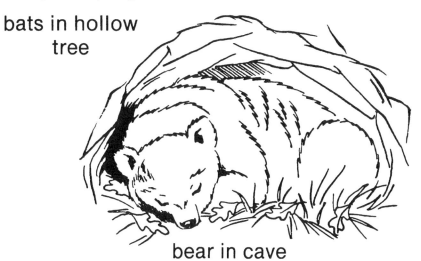

bear in cave

1. Name two animals that spend the winter in the bottom of a pond.

   _____ and _____

2. Circle the picture that shows the flying animal that hibernates in trees.

3. The animal that hibernates among the rocks is the _____ .

4. Name the animal that needs a large, protected place to sleep through

   the winter. _____

5. Circle your answer: Do people hibernate?   yes   no

Understanding Animals

Hibernation

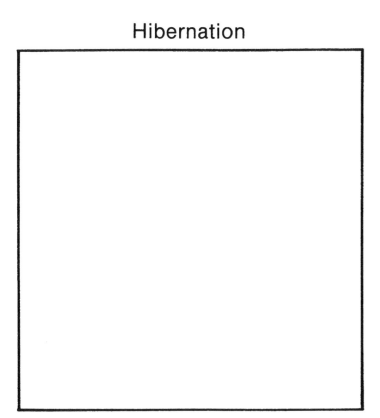

Circle the names
of animals that hibernate.
Draw a picture
of an animal hibernating.

turtle	deer
bear	snake
dog	bat
moose	lion
groundhog	frog

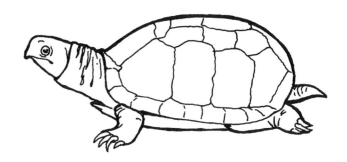

Circle the names of animals
that migrate.
Draw a picture
of an animal migrating.

duck	hummingbird
cow	wolf
seal	eagle
elk	snake
squirrel	salmon
butterfly	

Migration

Activities in Spring

Spring is a good time to do many things outdoors.

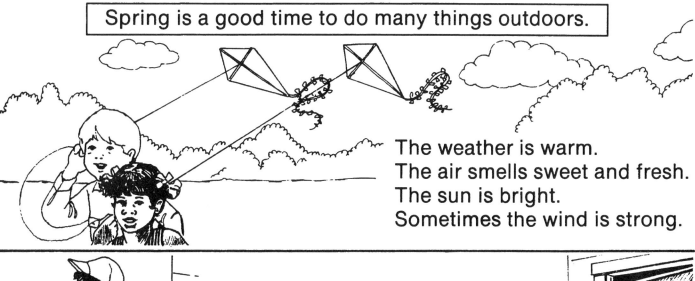

The weather is warm.
The air smells sweet and fresh.
The sun is bright.
Sometimes the wind is strong.

Things People Do in Spring

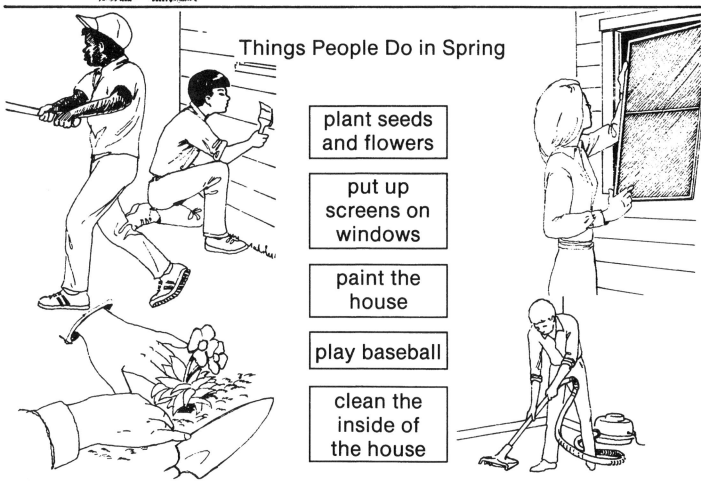

plant seeds and flowers

put up screens on windows

paint the house

play baseball

clean the inside of the house

1. Spring is a good time to fly a kite because the _____ is strong.
2. Draw lines to match the pictures with the boxes.
3. Circle your answer: Spring is a good time to clean up and fix up the house.   yes   no
4. Color all the pictures.

Activities in Summer

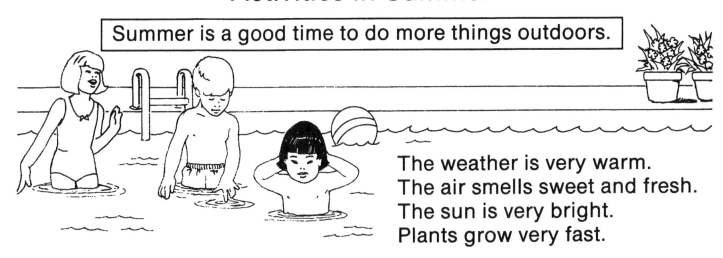

Summer is a good time to do more things outdoors.

The weather is very warm.
The air smells sweet and fresh.
The sun is very bright.
Plants grow very fast.

Things People Do in Summer

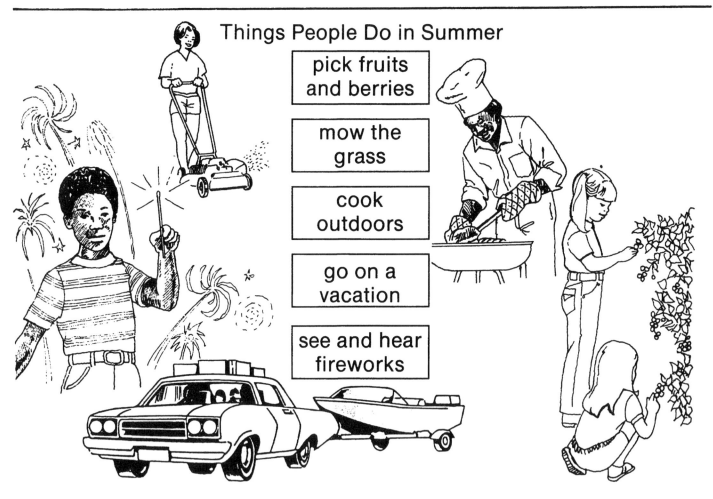

pick fruits and berries

mow the grass

cook outdoors

go on a vacation

see and hear fireworks

1. Summer is a good time to swim because the _____ is very warm.
2. Draw lines to match the pictures with the boxes.
3. Circle your answer: People do more things outdoors in winter than in summer.   yes   no
4. Color all the pictures.

Activities in Fall

Fall is a good season to do some things outdoors.

The weather is cool.
The sun is not very bright.
The leaves change color.

Things People Do in Fall

rake leaves

put up storm windows

play football

make a jack-o'-lantern

1. Fall is a good time to hike in the woods because the _____ have changed _____ .
2. Draw lines to match the pictures with the boxes.
3. Color all the pictures.

Activities in Winter

Winter is the season to do few things outdoors.

The weather is very cold.
Day is shorter than night.
Sometimes snow falls.

Things People Do in Winter

shovel snow

dress warmly
for outdoor fun

play ice hockey

put on
snow tires

have a New
Year's Eve party

1. Winter is a good time to ice-skate outdoors because water turns to
_____ when the weather is very _____ .
2. Draw lines to match the pictures with the boxes.
3. Circle your answer: Winter is the coldest season.   yes   no
4. Color all the pictures.

The Seasons

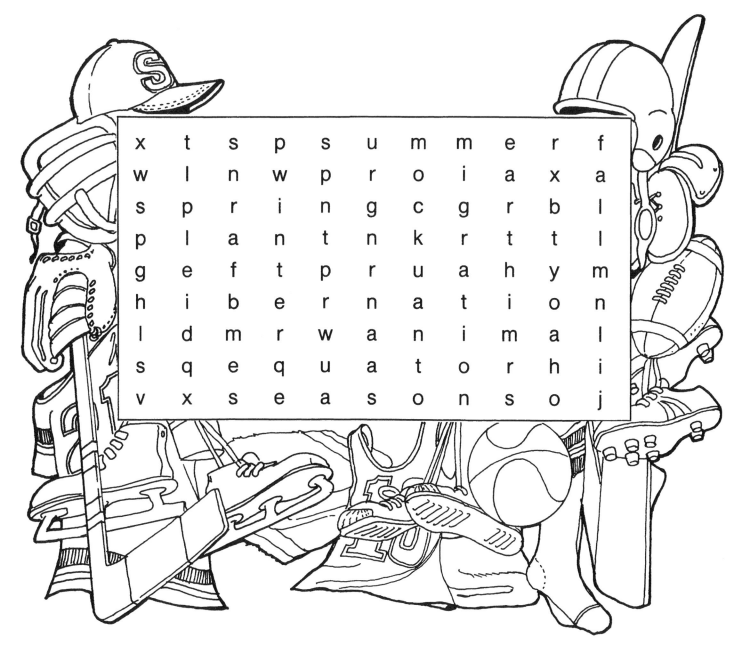

```
x  t  s  p  s  u  m  m  e  r  f
w  l  n  w  p  r  o  i  a  x  a
s  p  r  i  n  g  c  g  r  b  l
p  l  a  n  t  n  k  r  t  t  l
g  e  f  t  p  r  u  a  h  y  m
h  i  b  e  r  n  a  t  i  o  n
l  d  m  r  w  a  n  i  m  a  l
s  q  e  q  u  a  t  o  r  h  i
v  x  s  e  a  s  o  n  s  o  j
```

Circle these words in the puzzle.

Word Bank

winter	equator	seasons	animal
spring	earth	fall	plant
hibernation	migration	summer	

People spend the most time outside in _____ .

Some things that people do during this season are _____

_____ .

Animals During the Seasons

Look at the animals.

Think about how they act during the summer and during the winter.
Cut out the pictures.
Paste the animals in the right boxes.

Summer		Winter	